METAPHYSICS IN THE FOREST

POEM

ANDREW HAWTHORNE

*To Mary and Pete,
with best wishes,
Andrew*

THE LITTORAL PRESS

First Published 2006

The Littoral Press
38 Barringtons, 10 Sutton Road,
Southend-on-Sea, Essex SS2 5NA
United Kingdom

British Library Cataloguing-in-Publication Data:
A catalogue record of this book is available from
the British Library

ISBN 0-9550926-3-9

Cover Photograph: Clare Harvey

Printed by 4 Edge Ltd. Hockley, Essex, England

CONTENTS

For my Fathers in God in the Church of England: David King, Julian Hubbard, James Tarr, Bill Croft, Michael Fuller, Roger Watts, Graham Reeves, Michael Gudgeon, Hugh Williams, Gerald Harris, Alan Sessford, Robin Johnson, Bryan Apps and Alex Smith, and in Memory of Michael Lowe and John Colebrook, who baptised me but died before I came to faith.

> 'The Kingdom of God is as if someone would scatter seed on the ground, and would sleep and rise night and day, and the seed would sprout and grow, he does not know how.' *Mark 5:26-27*

And, as always, for Ceri and Emilia, who mean more to me than I can ever express in mere words.

CHRISTUS REX

Reformation

I Thomas Cranmer

staring into the embers of his hearth-fire
in the study lets the ink dry on the quill,
the last of the ink that the monks of Hailes
ground for him from gathered oak galls
and pigs' blood.

The pages in the ancient missal brought from his library
turn like desiccated leaves from autumns years before,
powdery at his touch, fox'd, smeared and smoothed
by anonymous fingers before him; yet

the black ink still cleaves there, and the gilt
and the lapis lazuli crushed and painted
with a single hair, these remain,
deep as the ocean.

In the dying crimson of the oak logs
seasoned at Lambeth in his garden there
he sees his own fire kindling,
fires, he prays, of purification,
the gold that might be his soul
and the leaf of the manuscript before him,
rendered and redeemed.

II Lancelot Andrewes

at prayer hears the cathedral clock
toll four, and underneath his study window
the matins thrush begins his music, weaving
with the bishop's whispered litanies
a divine antiphonary over the lawns.

His fingers on the ancient missal
trace with arthritic determination
illuminated letters whose gilded forms
he knows mostly now by memory, his eyes
become dim. The lapis lazuli and emerald
crushed with exemplary care and mixed and applied
so many years before by anonymous monks here
glint in the sun's first rays;
he remembers the miraculous depths
of colour on the page,
its vividness despite the years,
its smoothness under his thumb.

III Thomas Ken

in exile, regrets the moated palace,
the swans gliding to his proffered bread
at the ringing of the old sanctus bell
hung there for this purpose; his vaulted private chapel
where with the offering of sequestered incense
the prayers and hymns would come in visitation
like butterflies through a summer's window
and he'd scribble them down in the note-book
kept ready in his pew for this purpose,
letting them lie there through the day, proving
like bread, examining them after *Magnificat*
each evening, having his secretary copy out
the best of them then sending them
to his Lord the King in dedication.

Here instead swans are fit meat for table,
fetch good prices secretly at the barbarous market.

He dreamt, one night during a storm,
that at his death
four crowned swans and seven with mitres
bore his catafalque to heaven
across the waters, still as the moat,
and a choir of seraphim behind an arras veiled
chanted his hymns to tunes which
he could still remember in the morning,
Deo Gratias.

IV John Cosin

alone, so he thought, in the garden room,
tries the verses of his new hymn
across the roses growing outside his open window.
His servant, Michael, at his dusting
of his master's books,
his Monday duty after matins, starts,
rises from his knees, stands attendant
at the Bishop's side and,
realizing he's not been summoned,
begins to nod his head to the ancient beat
translated from the Latin.

Cosin finishes. He changes a word
in the middle of line six for the sake of euphony,
just like the rose he had the gardener move
by the old priory wall, for the sake of harmony.

The scent of the rose garden drifts across his desk
like the incense from the old services
in chantry chapels in his cathedral.

He pauses at the dedication,
watches the gloss of the ink dry off the parchment;
he glances suddenly to his left, sees
the embarrassed look of devotion withdrawn,
writes, *For Michael.*

V William Laud

in his cell wakes to the cries of the carpenters
below him in the square and the hammer blows
which reverberate like musket shots.
His scaffold nears completion. The block
has arrived, rough-hewn from a single oak,
his guard says, that pre-dated the faith in this land,
a pagan block for a popish prelate,
the Lord be praised.

That last day the workmen with adzes carve
two grooves each side for his head. He sees
the shavings pile up on the platform,
drying and curling in the heat
like September leaves, lighten,
drifting in the wind under the railing.

That night, his last, spent in vigil,
with psalms muttered from memory
deep into his cloak, he is visited
by visions of his blood, his dying crimson,
soaking into the oak, in runnels
finding the shavings, reinvigorating them,
making them appear like little tongues of flame.

THREE MONASTERY POEMS

The Abbot

in his oak-panelled study above the quire
had the lay brother, at the time for vespers,
place his chair over the central crossing
which arched below the floor-boards of his cell.

Here he'd found in his isolation
that the pine planks vibrated
to his brethren's chanting
and travelled up the oak frame of his abbots' throne
and into his soul and echoed there,
exultets and *glorias* finding room there,
in the silence of his world finding voice there,
his fingers tracing blindly in his breviary
each versicle and response, his own voice
(he hoped) keeping time, pitch and rhythm.

The Lay Brother

waits in the corner, silently out of custom
not necessity, and watches the Abbot's fingers
scrabble over the ancient breviary like crayfish
in a rock pool. He keeps time more or less

though the breviary is turned to the wrong place.
The Abbot keeps perpetually the feast of Corpus Christi
and his finger-tips have rubbed off the gold leaf
and lapis lazuli from the illuminated text.
His thumbs and fingers these days

are bejewelled, returning light to light
from the candle I carry as I put him to bed,
he still chanting the psalms for compline.

The Librarian

sits in the same cloister alcove where as a postulant
by charcoals and slate he'd learnt by heart the *Pater Noster*.
He is rebinding books, today the Abbot's festal Psalter
which has been worried free of its spine
by successive prelates' anxious fingers in the Quire
and blackened at the page-corners for three centuries.

The new kid leather, evenly stretched on its frame,
beside him on the bench, gleams white after its lime curing
and seems to him like a vast gull's wing in the morning air.
The silk thread he pulls through the bone needle coruscates
in the sunlight, flashing brief, tiny rainbows on the walls
and the gold tooling already applied glints as he turns it.
Inside the back cover, knowing it will be covered by the binding,
to a future craftsman who like him will sit here one day
and refurbish the Abbot's prayer book
when this present work is worn through, he writes,
'Benedict, by the Grace of God Librarian, greets you,
Binder, in the name of the Lord.
Though I be dust and ashes now,
pray for me, brother.'

A GLASTONBURY SEQUENCE
In the Year of Our Lord, 1539

II - Preparing the ink

Abbot Richard Whiting stands at the scribe's right shoulder,
as before, and supervises the grinding of the burnt swan's bone
and himself drips the antimony and charcoal tincture
to the right consistency, pestle and mortar
smoothing each droplet into the black paste
which with brandy mixed
and a quarter measure of swine's blood
produces the silky, creamy ink the Abbot favours,
which looks like sunlight shining through red wine
in an autumn goblet.

II - Preparing the vellum

The vellum once scraped and cut and stretched on the new frame,
once dried and flattened with the broad iron used only
for the Abbot's parchments and his surplices and albs

is set and pinned on his writing desk
like a vast wing of a lepidopterist's specimen.
Whiting tests its smoothness with the edge of his thumb
like a sculptor gauging the keenness of a favourite chisel.

The scribe then brings the new-cut quill
and the shimmering ink in a glass file
that Whiting for a flashing moment
likens to his Saviour's blood, fresh caught.

III - The Letter

'To my most High and Liege Sovereign,
by the Grace of God, Henry, King and Friend:'
     Whiting in his own hand,
slightly crabbed by arthritis setting in to the hair-line
fractures where his thumbs broke in a dormitory brawl
aged twelve, adds a flourish to the 'd' of friend
and hopes to catch and hold in the twirling spiral
of the floret, like a bluebottle in a spider's web,
some fine memory of that summer spent together,
tented in the Field of Gold, Henry's bonhomie then,
his hand on mine as we entered the lists, young men
in their ups, swapping Latin obscenities
about the King of France's arse.

IV - The Letter continued

'I, Richard Whiting, by God's appointment
Lord Abbot of Glastonbury, Canon of Gloucester,
Rheims and Milan, Priest: Greetings and Remembrances.'

     He the King is ill-advised,
led like a hind by wolves
through a summer's day clearing
in a dark wood.
The King's *mal* friends are fair-weather cavaliers
quick to ride on a firm path only
quick to snap at crumbs from the Royal plate
well placed to snatch the choicest sweetmeats too.

They are horseflies weaving deformed parabola
around a chained stallion
false pilots in unnavigable sounds,
treacherous vine-dressers who cultivate belladonna
in the physic garden of a blind man.

'We beseech thy Gracious Majesty of thy Clemency
to spare our House of Prayer which adorns thine lands
like the jewels thy crown.'

Whiting leaves the scribe to complete the rest,
his fingers aching. The usual arguments are rehearsed,
as at the monthly tithe gatherings at the Abbey door
with the local farmers. Scripture and tradition foremost,
then the infirmary, the care of orphans, widows,
and the school; the tide of paganism that always threatens
to swamp this Isle of Avalon like the March floods.
The Abbey's defences against these, too.

V - The gallows

The feet of Whiting's corpse, strung from the gate-house,
snagged like wayside brambles on the tumbrels
of the King's Commissioners
as they looted the library, the cellar,
and the Abbot's furniture.

Once quartered, Whiting's body
was delivered to all four reaches of the county.
The haunch that went to Wells
was delivered to the Bishop's Palace
just like the weekly venison, accompanied
by the Abbot's oaken throne
for which the Bishop paid thirty one florins,
believing it, *Deo Gratias*, to be a bargain.

God

I

God tapped me on the left shoulder one day
and handed me a leaflet advertising his garage sale.
'Hoarded too many things too long,' he said.
'Spread the word.' Then he was off to Lambeth,
he said, to ask his mate the Archbishop for a fiver
for his fare home. I heard later
he was given a quid and a cup of tea.

II

The Lambeth pound
conveyed him as far as Blackfriar's.
He spent the night in a bus shelter at Canongate.
He got as far as Croydon
by thumbing a lift from a passing
archangel who was glad of the company.
He roamed the streets until dark and found
the bus shelters there identical,
more or less.

III

He hitch-hiked to Brighton
over the South Downs
in a cattle-truck converted for hunting dogs.
'I drive,' said the driver, misquoting Wilde,
'the illegal for the indelible.'
'And the irremediable,' added God
with a chuckle that was swept out of the open window
over the chalk landscape like seeds from a dandelion clock
which lodged
somewhere on the scarp side of the Devil's Punch Bowl
and sprouted, eventually, wild strawberries and thyme.

IV

The beach at Brighton had more pebbles
than his old friend Abraham has descendants.
One or two more, actually. God dipped his toes
in the water, withdrew it quickly, decided
that the greenhouse effect wasn't such a bad thing,
after all. 'Ozone is over-rated,' he told
the ice-cream salesman who, much to God's amazement,
was called Adam.

V

But the sea, the sea,
he was proud of the sea.
Never still, never silent,
as broad as my mind but with more fish, God mused.

It is as it always was,
does what it always did,
consumer and begetter of land,
fruitful beyond all measures,
conveyer of warmth, fertility,
yet sterile, uninhabitable, almost.

He dipped in his toe again.
'It's not so bad, really,' he told a passer-by,
'Once you've got used to it.'

BIBLICAL FIGURES

Lazarus at table

I

is asked, again, by the visiting faithful
as they break his bread together over their cups,
to say something of those days.

Christ's tears, he says, it was these brought me forth
like a dormant tuber out of the winter tilth
its first shoot bone-white, disturbing the parched soil
like a dead-man's finger.

II

The darkness that clutches like
a wild beast, wolf, a lynx, in the night-time
the darkness that clings to your every fold
like smoke from a hearth-fire
the darkness that oozes into your soul
like spilt oil in fissures in the granite
the darkness

III

The cold sheer and absolute like fire
the cold that sucks out your soul
like wine from a perforated gourd
the cold that claims you as a dead tree
is claimed by the earth

The coldness,
darkness,
alone, alone, alone,
alone.

Moses

In his cups after the Passover remembers
the grimace of the dying Egyptian soldier
into whose heart he'd thrust his paring knife
as if into a water-melon. The dull
thwock as the blade pierced the rib-cage,
the silent fall of the corpse
like a stork brought down by an arrow,
slipping its perch on an oasis palm.

Abraham

At the altar of sacrifice raised the knife
and saw reflected in its burnished blade
an old man's face gnarled and striated
like the burl of an ancient olive tree.
Its new shoots
wan and tender like rhubarb under a cloche
would shatter under a late frost, die
budless, fruitless.

Job I

The earth trembled and shattered
like fissured ice
the sky spat ash and hailstones
smoke billowed and plumed
sulphur bubbled from fractures in the soil
the air boiled

God spoke.

Job II

'And what is this handful, this harvest of dust?
Pilgrim amidst the heath and heather and the heathen
companion of hermit-thrush and hibiscus?
His tongue I formed of ashes and embers
and atoms brazed in the fires of dying stars
before his world began. His soul I gave space to,
light to, grace to, when he was sealed in the womb.
His mind I expanded and by my own wit expended.
He is but dust and emptiness.
I will hear him.'

St Francis

I

deep in his prayers like a hind in the forest
feels the rough stone beneath his knees
and imagines the red wheals that will remain there
past lunchtime. And the motes of grit that will have
worked their way beneath his skin as he swayed
in trance; these he'll scrub away next bath day.

The marks of prayer, true prayer,
as the angel taught him under his torn wings,
remain after the last Amen. Like the rash on his neck
and arms from the cassock he had made
from the flour sacks.

II

When his stigmata pulsed and burned
he knew it was time to withdraw, silently,
from the presence of God
like Moses from the Mountain or
the hill fox from the carcass when the lynx appears.
When the marks of Christ beat in tune
with his own heart he knew the time
the time
time

St Benedict

in his cell knew the time for Terce
by the shadow the window bars made on his prie-dieu.
When they began to slant across the top left-hand corner
of his hand-written breviary
and bisected the 'O' of *Orates* he knew the oratory
should be filling with prayers
like lovers' sighs after consummation.
Rising as quickly as his hearth-servant knees permitted
he crossed himself, and his hand, arthritic,
cast a shadow on the lime-washed wall
which always reminded him of a dove
ascending.

St Dominic

at his desk turns the vellum pages of Augustine's 'City of God'
said by the librarian to be the Master's own copy, *Deo Gratias*.
Dominic's thumb and forefinger tremble
as they touch the grimy page corners as Augustine before him.
The page crackles as he turns it
like the red admiral's wing he plucked
out of the spider's web when he spring-cleaned the chapel
last Corpus Christi. Both surfaces slightly dusty,
the butterfly scales leaving a patina on his fingers
that he let remain there for days, as he will the touch
of this paper.
And outside in the cloister garth the lay brothers' chatter
at their gardening become in Dominic's rapture
the heathen army sent against Roman Hippo,
their rakes and shovels' clatter the Goth
swords and spear rattle,
and in each illuminated letter the crushed ruby
the faithful's blood.

St Teresa of Lisieux
On the photograph of her doing the washing-up

Teresa of the Dishes looks up momentarily
as the photographer calls her, softly, snapping
the famous picture of a saint in service, her dove-white hands
miraculously smooth like the plaster statue of Mary
in the ante-chapel. Flustered, she slops
some water over her habit, where the fading cloth
is fleetingly darkened and restored to the pristine jet-black
she marvelled at as she knelt and took her life-vows.
And on the cloth she sees in the subsiding soapsuds
a thousand images of her own face reflected,
and knows them as the face of Christ.

John Henry Newman
at his desk in his rooms in Oriel College, Oxford

takes from the locked draw the rosary
that arrived this morning in the post from Rome
like the dove that brought Noah his green sprig.

Sandalwood, he guesses by the aroma
rising like incense from his fingers
as he counts his prayers. Each bead
a prayer sent off to God, each bead
smooth and shining like the delphinium seeds
he remembers planting in the garden as a child.
Then the waiting, the expectation
of miraculous growth, the explosion of colours
like a rainbow sprouting from the dark soil.

E B Pusey

in his Hebrew grammar, enraptured by 10 o'clock
as always, is disturbed by the cathedral clock
and his Scout placing his coffee-cup
by his inkwell. The chink of the stirring spoon

coincides with the clock chimes, as always.
He mutters 'thank you', in Hebrew,
but Edgar is used to that, withdraws silently,
steps sideways and opens the study window
momentarily to let a trapped bee outside.

He watches it disappear over the quadrangle,
a tiny dot diminishing in the distance.

John Keble in 1858

in his garden cuts back the dogrose briars
that have overgrown of late the doorway
to his summerhouse. Within, the stifling heat
has rarified the air, and the rose blossoms
that have forced their way inside through
broken panes and ill-fitting lintels
have scented the room like Newman's incense
in his Oratory.

These Keble leaves, knowing that they like God's grace
will find the gaps and fissures in our lives,
break through and flower.

The missal

lies open on the altar, the corners
blackened by the fingers of innumerable priests
now bones in the church-yard. Its pages
brittle as I turn them, like
the desiccated wings of dead butterflies
caught long ago in spiders' webs
in the church hall.

On the unveiling of a plaque to Percy Whitlock

Organist and Composer, for many years Borough
Organist in Bournemouth, died shortly after giving
a concert at the town's Pavilion in 1946. He was 42.

After his last concert he steps
out of the auditorium and surveys the sea.
Its limitless horizons soothe his agitated soul,
- the rationing privations, the lack of paper
for his scores, the disappearance of his evening concerts -
and reminds him that his own music
like the waves' beat
like the returning shore after the tide
will outlast him, will echo with the pulse
and passion of him, this frail flesh,
to those to whom he will be a name
and a grave only, two words, three, only,
Percy Whitlock, Composer.

Laurence Bowman, Vicar of this Parish 1790-1827

Through his study window the Vicar at his prayers
could hear the song-thrush disturbing
the autumn debris around the roses in his shrubbery,
hunting worms and grubs and snails
under stones
and under the lintel and the Virginia creeper
that wound itself up the drainpipes.

Providence, he saw, stalks daily and substantially
these rounds and directs each molecule of soil
each breath of creaturely existence,
draws each dying prayer from his lips.

The priest on pilgrimage

The thin pages of his breviary rustle
like dried-out leaves as he turns them.
Matins, Terce and Sext, these are counted
and released on his breath into the air
like butterflies from the botanist's net. Psalms
and antiphons and canticles drift upwards
like smoke; from their wings
flash sapphires and emeralds out of the light.

The Vicar takes evensong

The congregation turn the pages to follow the service.
The paper's rustle sounds to him
like the flurry of birds' wings,
roosting or rising, either, and when he turns
in each palm there sits a dove or a cockerel,
an angel or eagle, and these same

sat there the days of England's perils
when the good Kings passed and when
the drone of enemy bombers overhead
drowned out the *Magnificat*
and when the threat of revolution and revisions
drew near the church council.

He'd seen them all, and lived,
prospered even,
and God's promises remained,
thin like the paper at his finger tips, certainly,
browned by successive generations at the corners,
but abiding.

An evening hymn
after the Phos Hilaron

O holy light of God the Father's glory,
  reigning in majesty,
clothed in splendour like the evening star, O Christ,
  thee we praise.

O Ancient Wisdom from on high, Lord Jesus
  forgive our sins, mercy
divine was never so sweet as this, in all eternity.

O Root of Jesse, David's Key, blessed Saviour
  send thy Holy Spirit
over all thy people, our sacred work to aid,
  perfect in thee.

Thou Corner Stone of our strong tower, with angels
  graced in thy pure love
protect us through this night, that we may rise
  at tomorrow's dawn
and offer thee our morning sacrifice of praise.

A hymn to Christus Rex
'The lowly Cross becomes the gilded throne'

Hail Holy Christ, reigning in splendour,
nailed to the Cross, your glory shines forth.
You have redeemed us, Satan has fled away,
Jesus, saviour of Israel.
Behold thy throne, gilded in holy blood,
angels attendant, crowned by the dove.
Spear, nails and thorns are your royal sceptres
wielded in love, in mercy transformed,
that in the Father's eternal Kingdom,
heaven and earth might be made one.

Advent

The twilight season came, the death of earth
and flesh and the people huddled
and my neighbour put up flashing Christmas lights
and the giant inflatable snowman
on top of his conservatory and dressed
as Santa Claus to please the children. But
will the Christ come, O my people?

BENEATH THE TREES

New Forest walking
December 2005

The forest plain, heather and bracken bedded,
gorse-strewn and studded,
the heather white in its winter skeleton
stretches away from us, fugitive, as the sun sets
and the mists begin in the hollows
where the puddle-ice creeps. The sun
briefly flames the water and out
of its loamy depths fires
quick jewels in its dying rays, ruby,
diamond; these are caught in the ice

as this moment is sealed in our memories,
hand in hand as we walk, the heather
catching at our feet, eager to keep us,
quell us and fix us
in significant soil.

Beneath the trees

We walk beneath the forest canopy
where silver birches puncture the March sky
like denuded whale ribs left on the beach,
bleached white in the sun, the waves out of reach
with their salt-raftered grave. Empty oak trees
depict both the model of blood vessels
in human brains and, in cankers, what ails
us, illness of aged limbs, backs and knees
while Scots pine sift the spring air with branches
like the lung's filigree. We are entranced;

life is reflected in the trees, season's
growth and dereliction, the blood and bone
of us, memory, affection and reason,
too brief: they'll remain when we are gone.

Late morning in the forest

The sun drips down, beats like globules of cream
from these trees, splashes among dead leaves,
disturbs them. In the forest canopy beech and oak crowns
flare into enormous jewels, oceans
and lakes out of the light. The morning
is down on its knees; the afternoon
crouches, ready to take fire.

Under the shelter of bracken and gorse
the scuttling creatures - dormouse and squirrel,
stag beetle and sand lizard - take their noon refuge,
the hour of sitting in your own shadow;
the noise of their retreat dissipates in the slight breeze.

Metaphysics in the forest

A lone tree on the skyline
silhouettes a model of the blood vessels in the brain.
Thoughts, affections, and conceits;
dead leaves underneath.

October walk through the woods

Frost-fall slices through the late afternoon
like the leaves which scythe through the air
and settle on your hair and shoulders and are
brushed away with laughter, the sunlight
picking gilded filigree out of stray strands
as you shake your head. Our passage
disturbs the fractured leaves and twigs
and fungi on the forest floor; a sweet aroma
rises like the waft of incense in a deserted chapel
after vespers. We walk on.

Looking into the sun

in this forest we see the silhouettes of trees.
Substance is lost and their black forms triumph.
They become pure shadows of themselves,
unadulterated by tone and differentiation;
they are hard, soaring, primal. Across the leaf-strewn
floor they replicate themselves endlessly,
blur together, diffuse.

Waiting for a summer storm

The air hangs heavy beneath the leaves
like perfume on a prostitute. It hunches,
still and pregnant, and squeezes
the ants back to their nest, the crow
to its branch. The birdsong evaporates,
clouds coagulate, pass their shadows over the forest
like a priest's hands over the dying.
The first fat drops like gunshots
in the trees.

PILGRIMAGES

Deserted crofts
Malvaig, Wester Ross, August 1999

The sheep's home only, and
the autumn leaves decaying
where the wind left them. Under
enormous skies no different from the sea
the timber rots, leaving no trace
nor imprint in the granite bedrock.
The stone walls decay also, decline
into what they were before or else
form new homesteads with English brick
or a painted lintel or an unrecognisable hearth.
The moss thrives.
The bramble struggles upwards,
slips, its runners knot, entwine together,
produce unharvested fruit year by year.

Albert Einstein discovers
that the speed of light is constant

I

And then he knew that everything is
history. The past claims us, and again.
Light from the furthest star, the moon's waning,
passing clouds, his maid's fussing with the dust
upon his books, his own breath as it blossomed
in the frosted air on his way to the privy,
all these at the moment he saw them
were moments already dead.
The past is all around us, behind us and before us,
like a river mist, inside us. There is no present
except in the mind's eye
and that he knew from the history of his own
nation's bones was a kingdom of darkness.
There was not now, not forever.

II

So he let his hair grow long, his whiskers too,
which went white before their time.

Love out of sight

Our eyes following the squirrel we disturbed
find near the crowning branches of the beech tree
indistinct initials carved in a heart in its bark.

Wartime lovers near the aerodrome here
with a penknife hand-in-hand entwining their lives
together for all to see as they sliced and scratched.
Sap ran, congealed, left its scent heavy on their fingers
and in an unmarked grave in Normandy.

The wounded tree recovered, prospered,
has now outlived them, and carried
their love steadily skyward.

A burial witnessed in Kanungu, Uganda
May 2005

Here we inter Peter, folding him into the earth
like the millet and maze he planted here
and his forebears before him, and with prayers
wish for him a good harvest. The terraced hills
around, the coombs and valleys rich
with a mantle of mango and tea, sweet potato,
banana and passion fruit, these welcome home
their son, their flesh and blood and bone and earth,
tiller of soil and maker of good red bricks,
and embrace him like a mother her child,
wombfruit, earth brother, and in them he becomes
the soil and the seasons in the soil. We send him
homeward, and we travel with him,
and he will be beneath us, around us and within us,
and the rains will seep him into the roots
and the tubers; he will return and come and go
and us along with him, perpetually.

The Creation of King William's Royal Forest

Here the farmsteads, homesteads, crofts
and cattle pens were torn down by men on horseback,
King's men with ropes and iron spears and parchment decrees,
destroyers of villages, hamlets, ings and enclosures
where the soil was tamed and significant.
Here the thatch and furze burned
here the horseshoe stamped its *imprimatur*
of destruction and desolation, populations
moved like condemned sheep to the sea coasts
and the foreign ways of fishing.

The King went riding, then, over
undulations in the earth where houses were razed
to their post-hole bones, over hummocks of chapels
and privies, over the new grass where the boar roamed,
over forgotten graves where tibia and skulls
become soil.

Visit

Three faces around my bed, looking over me.
Three angels of the Trinity, perhaps, like
Rublev's icon in my study,
or toads. Three toads crouching.
They mutter and gibber like a mountain beck
babble over protruding rock
wipe away tears,
touch my hand,
refuse to leave.

They rearrange the flowers.

Connie's Conkers

Mrs Radcliffe until the October she died
collected conkers from the chestnut tree
her father had planted the day she was born
and offered them like sweets in a bucket by the gate
for passing generations of school children.

The tree had weathered every storm with her,
crouched through the blitz with her,
flowered and budded and bore fruit with her

the frail, hard, shiny fruit that slipped
one day too soon from the shell of her and
was buried quietly in the overgrown
corner of the cemetery next to the suicides.

Connie's conkers started many school-ground fights,
many wars, many bruised knuckles
and stolen shoe-laces for strings

and for their grave lay shattered and bruised
in playground and gutter, in the bottom of satchels,
gnarled and dried, as grooved and worn
as her own hands as the years wore on.

She fell, one autumn, her life's husk
split and cankerous.
The conkers that year were the last offered
and in subsequent seasons they stayed where they fell.
Some flourished and took.

The Ascent of Macchu Pichu

I A stinking bus

They hadn't told her at Thomas Cook
that this back-pack trek would sacrifice
three days in a stinking bus. Nicotine
and hair-grease streaked the windows,
some blood also, she noted.

Culcupalpa and San José passed in quick
terra-cotta brushstrokes hastened by an artist
whose soul had already left when he set up his easel.

Children's hands lifted, palms suppliant
or waving goodbye, she could not tell.

On their faces, blurred as they were by the speed,
history had scoured unforgiving lines,
eyes which had seen her before, it seemed.

II At Atamempa they stopped for food

At Atamempa their dust cloud trailed in their wake
at last caught up with them. On settling, it lightened
most faces but darkened hers. She would soon be used to it,
recognising its faint ring round her clothes on the floor
where she undressed,
and prompting memories when she found it still
in her compact months later in the office.

She learned to wash the fruit from the roadside stalls,
the dust they had brought with them behind the bus
turning to quick mud at her feet,
the pomegranates and peaches left
glowing in her hand.

III Discarding the phrase book

She also learned that her phrase book was useless
when she tried to piece together from the syllable rubble
of their chatter more than one word at a time.
Their grunts and murmurs were the grey shale
on the passing mountains, to her
obscuring the bedrock of their language
and permitting no foothold. When they saw her

discard the book their voices grew louder
and she heard the rattle of their ancestor's bones
on their rolling tongues in stories polished
and perhaps embellished at each telling, either
the rape and murder, the white slave gatherers,
eyes fallen for the gold, blood
on their hands and faces
the screams and the orphaned villages
where the crops rotted in the fields

or else the fettle of the trussed chickens between their feet,
the maze yield per hectare, or the price of Nike trainers.

Their clothes and beads looked the same in their infinite variety,
their black hair and walnut faces also.

IV A guide book kind of story

The passenger next to her suddenly animated.
He pointed with a crab hand at the picture in the guidebook
open on her lap, a small child cradled
by his mother in a doorway, the fresh earth turned mud
in the spring rain but hardening now in the morning sun,
a rash of purple bougainvillea and its scent heavy
after breakfast -
"A typical Andean village and inhabitants."

It was this same man, but thirty years ago, and
in agitated vowels and flailing hands and a clicking tongue
he was telling her the story of his mother's gentle touch,
his weak legs, her raven hair.

His mother was dead now but his father
still had cravings for Lucky Strikes,
waited for a hip replacement in the city, could tell you
his family history and a good yarn of the old days
when the mountains had dragons and gods, with a photograph
all for five dollars. Maybe four.

At the next stop she tore out her name from the front cover
and binned it.

V A view at the window
The view from the window
had been spectacular for three hours
but as the mountains grew even more rugged
and the engine wheezed and the chickens gasped
in the thinning air,
she became used to it. The ravines
though deeper just looked dirty, the snow black at the edges,
the discarded Pepsi cans glinting in the noon sun
which began to beguile her companions to their siesta.

VI Over the Mountain: Macchu Pichu from an ice-cream van

For them it did not seem what their forebears said,
the navel of the world,
but the chance for a piss behind the rocks
and a cold beer illicit from the ice-cream van.
This is what she had come for, she whispered.
She was the only one who strayed to the edge of the lay-by,
holding her skirts as she walked by the bus exhaust,
fumbling for her camera in her rucksack,
feeling a sense of distance and alienation
through lack of oxygen.

The cracked horn of the bus called her back.
As she turned she hoped her photos
would not be overexposed, stumbled a bit
over the loose stones, looked up and saw sixty faces
looking down at her, in what might have been pity,
or just puzzlement.

THE SEA, THE SEA

The sea

is scaled by the wind (moderate, variable)
like the vast grey-green back
of a fairy-tale dragon. Its ripples and waves
are tensing muscles, the surf-break on the beach
its teeth and claws and the endless crash
of water on rock
its soul-juddering screams.

In the ruins of St Catherine's Chapel
St Catherine's Hill, Christchurch

History here has a long half-life. Seasons
drift across these fallen stones
like waves across the granite ledges
off St Aldhelm's Head, the changes
over years imperceptible, microns.
Birch and elder search more diligently,
internecine roots scarfing to the foundation
of things, beyond. Brambles and nettles
flourish then recede on this thin soil,
smothering chiselled stone then revealing
collapsed arches, mullions, transoms, plinths.

Early morning on the beach

Last night's footprints on the sand,
picked out boldly by the rising sun,
are smoothed away by the rising tide

just like the limestone of the church
of St Peter-on-the-Cliffs, weathered and beaten
by successive storms and centuries.
Lovers have danced and tumbled at the waves' mouth,
left furrows and indentations and trodden
scallop shells as their evidence.

The church clock strikes six, releasing
from its Saxon tower a flurry of herring gulls
over the beach.

The sea, the sea
Southbourne Cliffs, Bournemouth

The sea, the sea, the limitless sea. Its tides and swells
conceal
continents beneath them, conquered lands
in plains and mountain ranges
and rifts and fissures that could devour
whole civilisations in abyssal void
where ships and aircraft and satellite debris
litter the ocean floor. Salt water and crustacea
reclaim them, dissolve them,
the water towers over them.

Passing keels overhead
flit by like the indescribable shapes
when you close your eyes against the sun.

Here the grass grows
Southbourne Cliffs, Bournemouth

Here the grass grows long, forgotten by the council
due to budget cuts. The memorial bench to Bill and Deirdre Crow
paid for by their absent sons subsides
beneath a rising tide of plantains, dandelion, burdock and
white nettle. Their solemn, stable ship of marriage
blessed for fifty years in these parts according to the bench's plaque,
is done for, has foundered in the deep sea swell, like the rest of us.

The wind stirs through the grass.
It ripples and tosses
like waves on the sea.

The mist
Southbourne Cliffs, Bournemouth

The mist sits heavy on the sea.
In the early morning sun, diffused,
the horizon lies cloaked
with suspended water on the waves.

A fishing smack chugs between the lobster pots,
hauls up either writhing claws or an emptiness
breaking water like a voided womb.
It cleaves the sea in its wake, or else the sky;
trawls for lobsters, kites, and herring gulls.

Purbeck through the mist

Is a whaleback in a glowering line
with Corfe Gap making a cupid's bow
in its chalk lip, half a kiss across the bay.

Swanage tumbles into the sea;
its white-decked houses resembling tombstones
in an abandoned cemetery.

Behind us on the Isle of Wight Tennyson Down
dips to the ocean floor. There is a whisper of music
in the wave-beat and the breeze in the grass.

A view of the Purbecks

St Alban's Head, fresh white in its chalk
like a sliced rib
like an extracted tooth
enfolds Swanage, hidden Corfe,
the castle ruins where the wrecked stone
seeks the oblivion of earth,
the good earth gone under the sea.

On its whale's back, flexing
like the warp of centuries, time itself,
the fields hunch and knuckle.
Human endeavour is lost here,
ploughed into the soil, loaming.
The ocean beats.

Hengistbury Head

Your crumbling sides
like a diary indifferently flicked through,
diminished by revelation.

Ancient driftwood,
a pottery shard,
a horde of shells

forgotten. At the tide's reach
yesterday's secrets
for the casual eye
written in the sand.

ON THE POETS

William Barnes takes his weekly walk into Dorchester to reset his pocket watch by the town clock

*Once a week the parson-poet William Barnes made this journey
into Dorchester. Max Gate is the house Thomas Hardy had built
in 1885, a year before Barnes' death.*

Sometimes walking into town on a Thursday afternoon
you would meet your neighbour Thomas Hardy.
If you could manage it this would be
with a wave from the other side of the road. Otherwise
you'd have to linger if you passed on the same path
and endure Hardy's monologues on his wonderful
new house which you regretted in this landscape

as bitterly as a foreign word on an English tongue.
Its newly painted Gothic gables did not suit your vision
of homely thatch; nor was there the scent
of a good hearth's smoke on Hardy's clothes and hair.
The plumbing, they said, was efficient also.

So you'd amble up South Street
sifting the vowels of the passers-by as you went,
measuring their smoothness
as a miller passes his hand through his flour,
sometimes leaving finger prints.

Under the clock tower you would reset the watch,
knowing beforehand by the season whether
it had lost or gained, three or four minutes,
no less, no more.

Then back to your own hearth, the gathering sundown,
passed All Saints' Church by the Bockhampton road
which slid you unnoticed round Max Gate,
and you counted the homeward thrushes and felt the clutch
of the bramble and bracken round your feet,
noted the dappled sun between the leaves of overhanging oak and elm,
enjoyed their intermittent shade.

And in the silence of the country air
you heard the whispers of the ancestors' dust within the stone
and underneath their brooding tumuli,
mingling broken vowels in desiccated tongues.

On your return you reset the mantle clock,
turn to your desk with its waiting lamp,
your hand-made paper and your home-cut pen.
You allow your heartbeat to settle after your exertion
to the rhythm of the clock, and let it beat
the rhymes and lyrics of your passing day
into a new poem, an offering like prayer.

Egdon Heath
Canford Heath, Poole, July 2005

Egdon Heath remains here, between the gravel-pits
and the crematorium.
The rest is built on.
Poole and Bournemouth have devoured it
with concrete and tarmac and out-of-town shopping malls.
Here is preserved, its gorse and heather matting the soil,
entwining and keeping. The ancient desolation thrives and squats here,
few traverse its pathways, the scars swathed across the heath
like sword-cuts in flesh, the bones and sinews beneath,
flint and chalk.

Mr Eliot walks on the Dorset Heath

A walk he took in October 1938 with Mary Trevelayan

I

He finds the earth beneath him
layered with early fallen leaves that cling
to his every foot-fall, stifling
sound and echo, the rustling of the wind
in the boughs above and his companion's chatter.
This season's fall still held a glimmer of summer green
within their curling ribs
but others were gleaming yellow or brown
and last season's were black and disintegrating
beneath them.

II

The gorse was brittle and the heather dimmed.
The rain is late this autumn and the fallen leaves
skitter over dusty soil. A lone cricket chirps
out of the stony silence.

Your hand in mine, how like the curling
of the leaves together as they fall, grasping
between them a slither of empty space
like the sigh of an old man on his death-bed.

Preparing the poem
R S Thomas instructs his followers

Go out to the cold, the frost-strafed fields
where the earth is crow-scratched and empty.
Stand by the edge of the ploughlines,
on the frost-scorched footpath
where the stones of the ruined chapel
are exposed every winter, where the trails
of fox and badger have cut a way. Then wait
and open your soul and taste its emptiness,
feel the winter death seep from the soil
to your own heart, and room there, then
speak and listen to the echoes.

Wordsworth's Year
Ambleside, August 1999

The stream in April reminded him
of a clavichord played by a girl in a white dress.
Its thin music was muslin and lace,
virginal, almost.

August grew rank, the brambles choked
and the thick weed made 'cellos of the water,
languid and deep. Its tune entered his soul,
found ample room there to echo.

October's mist played a shrouded requiem,
ghosts of old priests hereabouts with the scent of incense
and the faint whisper of plainsong attendant.
The leaves broke; their frail bones
seeped into the wet bank, or else
wept themselves back to the river.

The winter ice hid the music to all
but his ears. Behind its auditorium's closed doors
he sensed the rhythm of its flow,
guessed its movements, pauses, pulses, repetitions,
added his own accompaniment
with a pebble skimmed across its surface.

THE LIFE OF SIGNIFICANT SOIL

Ploughteam

The ploughteam drive the stavelines through the soil.
Ravens, rooks, crows and pigeons scrawl
over the ruts and ridges of earth;
parasites on our toil and fatigue, worn hands
and dust-streaked faces. Their caws and screeches,
delving after earthworms and chrysalises
and spent seed secured in the soil, become
the sharp music of autumn and spring, of frost-fall
and hearth-fire, of the ploughshare's blunting,
of sliced soil, the earth's skin scoured,
the unearthed tossed flint and stone axe-head,
thrown horseshoe, nail and bone-knob.

Spring at Maiden Castle

March brings scents
of primrose and hyacinth,
erupted sterile earth where the shoots break,
and last year's leaves corrupted
into a single loam.

Under the roots that clutch
the failed tuber weeping
next summer to the soil
the damp bones register the slightest tremor,
rabbit and badger disturbing their dead
with fresh burrows,
the rambler climbing unknown tumuli.

The people are restless.
The frost still fingers the window,
pond and ditches; beyond the window
the evenings yawn wider.

When a cloud passes

Shadows skating over the ground
like the mouth of a grave,
a dark door into the future.

The breeze-blown grasses, cowslips
and ground elder, these
experience briefly a quick-come night,
momentarily cease photosynthesis,
sleep.

Feathers

Swifts and starlings rise and fall under the clouds,
spar, chatter and dart. The air is full of them
like motes of dust in the sunlight.
Over the village, above the huddled thatch
and the rising smoke from a dozen fires,
stray feathers float, ascend on hidden thermals,
are buffeted on the breezes of a higher atmosphere,
are picked and fretted over the fields until
the setting sun and the cooler air
drops them to earth. There they are found
by mice and magpies, taken quickly,
incorporated as nests and birthing chambers.

A country walk

The blossom gathers. Hawthorn and elder bows
are picked in white like sun-bleached ribs.
Beached whales; crabs beneath. The tide advances.
Bees scurry, vibrate against unfurling leaves,

return mechanically across the fields
to their white hives. In the fields the furrows
tremble, crumble over barley shoots; soon the earth
will lie broken and flat
like the ocean bed. We wander aimlessly,
pick flowers, notice odd-shaped stones,
beach-combers tracing the tide's reach,
pass by.

Sunlight after rain

Puddles evaporate. The oil that sheened them
returns to cover the tarmac and concrete,
a grey film congealing out of polychrome veneer,
a rainbow's footprint.

Early morning in late August
Whatstandwell, Derbyshire 1999

Autumn soothes itself over the wet grass,
hints in river mists an early shroud,
dreams the fall of leaves in a gentle breeze
that rattles the silver birches.

In the churchyard the spiders' webs
are picked in the silver dew, telling
in broken skeins the passage of rabbit and squirrel
and the matins priest. Craneflies mimic
rising smoke in the early sun. Shadows
are cast by the damp headstones like doorways
into the rich earth. Their weathered inscriptions
are revealed by the slanting dawn,
long forgotten names offered briefly
like the fruit of the church-wall bramble.
They wither unharvested.

The Meadow

Chilbolton Common, Hampshire

The meadow in the evening dewfall
soaks our feet as if we'd waded in the surf,
the swaying grasses in the summer breeze
its whirls and eddies.

Our shadows precede.
Burdock and cow-parsley catch
and clutch at our shoes,
bramble and nettle distort our forms
as our shadows pass over them;
they ripple and reform.

September Days

The noon-tide sun sears the ripening fruit,
blackberry, rowan, elderberry and acorn.
They begin to collect, ungathered, beneath
bramble and bush, leaving stains
and indentations in the loam
where unheeding feet have passed.

This unhurried, pleasantly warm
death
seeps between the drying leaves, over
the agitated field mouse, the drooping bracken,
our lives.